# God,

# I Wanna Be

# An Actor!

# God,

# I Wanna Be

# An Actor!

SCOTT LAIRSON

Unless otherwise indicated, all Scripture quotations are taken from *the Holy Bible, New Living Translation*, copyright © 1996, 2004, 2007 by Tyndale House Foundation. Used by permission of Tyndale House Publishers, Inc., Carol Stream, Illinois 60188. All rights reserved.

Scripture quotations marked (NIV) are taken from *THE HOLY BIBLE, NEW INTERNATIONAL VERSION® NIV®* Copyright © 1973, 1978, 1984 by International Bible Society® Used by permission. All rights reserved worldwide.

Scripture quotations marked (AMP) are taken from the *Amplified Bible*, Copyright © 1954, 1958, 1962, 1964, 1965, 1987 by The Lockman Foundation. Used by permission.
Used by permission.

Published by XP Publishing
A department of Christian Services Association
P.O. Box 1017, Maricopa, Arizona 85139
www.XPpublishing.com

ISBN- 978-1-936101-45-0

Printed in the United States of America. For worldwide distribution.

# DEDICATIONS

I first want to dedicate this book to **God** Himself! It is because of the Father, the Son, and the Holy Spirit that I live, move, and have my being!

To my beloved wife, **Pat**, who provokes me in ways that put me into action. I love her for that and much more.

To my sister, **Donna**, who was there from the beginning of my career, thank you for your thoughts and insights, and your unconditional love.

To **Patricia King**, one of the most creative visionaries I have had the pleasure of knowing, the woman who has instilled in me the phrase, "If you can see it, you can have it!"

And to **all actors**, present and future, you must know who you are in GOD before you can know who you are as an actor!

# C O N T E N T S

Introduction

-13-

Creating Your Environment

-17-

Desire & Passion

-29-

Energy & Stamina

-35-

Determination & Resiliency

-41-

Self-Confidence

-49-

The Spiritual Aspect of Acting

-55-

Decrees for Actors

-69-

# FOREWORD

## Patricia King

God shocked me when He first asked me to enter the world of media back in 2003. No one could have been more surprised than me. I had never felt comfortable in front of a camera. Yet what does our personal comfort have to do with obeying an assignment the Lord places in our hand?

I was further surprised in May 2009 when He invited me to host a Film Festival and establish a professional acting school for the TV/film industry. I had watched very few movies in my life and knew nothing about the world of entertainment media. But, since when does ignorance give us excuse to disobey His mandates?

I have found that when you say "YES" to what God asks of you, you will never be disappointed. His grace truly is "amazing." In spite of my initial reservations, I have enjoyed this journey as God has led into areas of service that I never would have dreamt possible.

God is raising up a mighty media army in this hour, which includes a company of actors and actresses who will not be bought or sold into a system motivated by greed, self-promotion, and personal fulfillment. These 'called-out ones' are on a mission to exalt their God in an hour when the entertainment media has become the most influential pulpit in the world. Every movie, television program, or video clip preaches something–for good or for evil. That should motivate the Body of Christ to move into the realms of media to stake a claim for His glory.

Although few of the movies the Lord breathes on will openly preach the gospel message, they will share His heart and values subtly leading a world, desperately seeking "more," to the "abundant life" found only in Him. Certain committed believers are being called to stand behind this global pulpit of entertainment media.

You have picked up this book because you feel called to act and I bless you! You may not have realized it but your career desire is a Kingdom calling! For this reason, prepare well because you are not only fulfilling your desire but your calling.

Scott Lairson is a skilled and respected casting director with many years experience in Hollywood's television and film industry. He has God-given insight into what it takes for a Christian to become a good and successful actor. This book is full of practical, anointed words of instruction, encouragement, and exhortation that will give you the foundational building blocks required for your successful acting career and calling.

Pursue your dream to act with all your heart, mind, and strength and be blessed as you embark on this glorious journey!

Patricia King
Founder XPmedia
XPmedia.com

# INTRODUCTION

**W**hy did you pick up this book? Was it because you have always wanted to act or because someone asked if you had ever thought of being an actor? Perhaps you pondered the question, "Can actors really be Christians and still have an acting career?" The answer is an absolute YES! In fact, God is now calling people who will serve Him in this strategic arena. Actually, there are Christians in the field of acting already.

Hollywood and the entertainment industry have been a treacherous field in which to labor for Christians. Although it is perceived by on-lookers as a glorious and glamorous lifestyle, in all honesty, working more than 15 years in this field, as a casting director, I have seen many individuals destroyed by the bi-polar world of the entertainment industry. I know personally what it is like to face discouragement, rejection, loneliness, and lack of appreciation while attempting to find God's purpose in it all.

It is not enough to merely ask the Lord to bless your acting career; He must be the center of it if you are to reach the place He has prepared for you. It took me years to discover this and other truths about being a successful Christian in Hollywood and now I believe the Lord has asked me to pass these insights along to you.

So, this book is for you, the actor who wants to act but desires to have God at the center of it all, without making compromises. Your acting career will take many twists and turns but how you serve God with meaning and purpose must remain solid, it is everything! I have written this book with the sole purpose of enriching your aspirations of being a Christian who acts.

Take the plunge into acting but first, build a strong foundation of faith as you step into a fulfilling career. There is an entire world out there waiting for YOU — Ready! Set! Action!

# Your Script for Success

*It is not enough to merely ask the Lord to bless your acting career; He must be the center of it if you are the to reach place He has prepared for you.*

*You need to study and work on your craft. If you`re not prepared when that dream audition comes, you are not going to get that opportunity. To me, the definition of success is when opportunity meets preparation.*

**Hilary Swank ~ Actress**

# CREATING YOUR ENVIRONMENT
## (YES! IT WILL COST YOU SOMETHING)

**A**re you ready to turn your dream of acting into reality? Before you take an acting class, purchase headshots, or go for an audition, you need to lay the groundwork for your success. After being in casting in Hollywood for more than 15 years, I know and will share with you "tricks of the trade"— tools necessary for success — and give you an honest appraisal of the business and help you understand God's plan for your acting dream.

However, first …,

## DO YOU HAVE WHAT IT TAKES TO BE AN ACTOR?

Perhaps you had a cathartic moment while sitting in front of television or in the top row of the movie theater munching on your favorite snack or while watching the local Shakespearian Company perform Romeo and Juliet and you said to yourself, "I can do that!" However, the truth is acting takes more than a mere passing thought; it requires hard work and a forceful desire to complete the journey into an acting career.

Ask yourself how your acting goal harmonizes with your:

- Plans for your life?
- Plans for your family?
- What GOD has planned for you?

Life's journey is sequential; it runs the gamut of being emotional, psychological, physical and, above all else, spiritual. If you will candidly answer these questions before you begin, it will increase the likelihood of acting opportunities and the possibility of your survival, success, and satisfaction as you step into God's destiny for you.

Becoming an "actor" means far more than merely acting, performing, or playing a role. Successful acting is comprised of skill sets, instruction, creativity, flexibility, focus, instinct, the ability to adapt, and honesty. Good acting is a lifelong process through which an actor pursues opportunity, uses the acquired resources, and initiates change as their acting ability develops.

Success in an acting career is far from guaranteed and may depend on how you define it. Success to some may be getting work as an extra or a small part in a television show, on stage or in a film. Others may define success as becoming a series regular in a television show, the lead in a feature film, or becoming a celebrity so famous that the whole world knows them and their picture is on the cover of People or Star magazine! Whatever your idea of success may be, there is WORK INVOLVED!

## Actors Are Rarely Discovered at the Mall
## ~YOU NEED A PLAN~

If you're truly serious about an acting career, you need to create an environment for success. Here is a list of just a few of the many things you can do to begin creating that environment to prepare for your acting career.

- Take classes in acting, singing, dance, voice, movement, and other TV and film workshops.
- Read books about the industry.
- Subscribe to and read entertainment industry trade papers.

- Attend film festivals, screenings, plays, movies etc.

- Visit websites and social networks to keep updated about the industry.

- Join social networking groups that help you make the right contacts.

Everything you do should help support your vision of becoming an actor and forward your career. The possibilities are unending, but whatever you do, wherever you look, your environment must support your goals to help you achieve success. That includes your relationship with GOD, your networking, your physical environment, your finances, and the way you take care of yourself. Creating your acting career environment is not easy, but once set up it will be much easier to manage your dream. Just make certain that you do not skip this step!

When I came to Hollywood many years ago, I came with a purpose and a goal. I knew that with my background and experience as the managing agent of a small talent agency in Ohio, I could take my training and abilities to the next level, the position of casting director. So, I packed up my bags, moved to Los Angeles, called my few connections, and started on my journey. IT TOOK TIME, *many* phone calls and interviews, and GOD opening the doors for me to make it. I started as an assistant to one of the top casting directors in Hollywood. Only with time—lots of hard 12-hour workdays and several casting assistant jobs—did I achieve the title of "Casting Director." For over 15 years in Hollywood, I worked with some of the top actors, producers, directors, and other casting directors in the industry. I discovered they ALL had two things in common: they had set goals for themselves and created environments that led to their success!

> "For I know the *plans* I have for you," declares the LORD, "*plans* to prosper you and not to harm you, *plans* to give you hope and a future."
> Jeremiah 29:11
> (NIV- emphasis added)

You must *plan* and create an environment for GOD to bless your acting dreams. GOD has big *plans* for you as an actor; as HIS created being, you were made to create too. So first, create your acting career environment so that GOD can come and prosper your *plans*!

## Do You Have the Right Stuff?

Let's look at what it takes to succeed in this business and answer the questions: Can all actors be successful? And, where does your talent fit into the process?

What is *talent*? Everyone who chooses to act believes they have talent on some level. We are all equally valuable to GOD but not equally gifted. Some people seem to be blessed with a multitude of talents—they can act, sing, dance, write, and direct—apparently able to do it all, while most actors will have only one or two talents. If it's your dream or calling to be an actor or obtain some other position in the entertainment industry, you must develop the talent(s) and gift(s) GOD has given you.

I have cast and come to know successful celebrities and actors who have been in the business for years, yet many

## Important:

*Your talents, regardless what your family and friends think, are probably not going to be enough! Who is the more likely to become successful, the person who relies on their raw talent alone or the person who recognizes all their talents and develops them? The answer is obvious. All of the brilliant actors you see on television or in films, and even the celebrities everyone knows have ALL DEVELOPED their talents and skills rather than solely relying on untrained talent.*

of them still have acting coaches and some even continue to attend acting classes. The only person that can stop your development as an actor is you! What makes the difference between being a talented or a mediocre actor? It comes from the choices you make. The key choices you make, apart from the natural talent you already have, will set you apart from others who have talent alone. We always have a choice. Even when it seems there are no options, there is always something we can do to improve ourselves.

Most of what happens in our lives is the result of choices and decisions we make. The destiny GOD wants to bring you into as an actor with a career in acting is not a matter of chance, it is a matter of choices; it's not a thing to wait for, but an outcome to be achieved—like our relationship with GOD. We can't wait for God to force a relationship on us, we have to choose to have one and pursue it.

You may "call" yourself an actor but if you "choose" to be an actor, you must be ready to count the cost and put in the time and effort, not just financially, but physically, spiritually and emotionally. Shakespeare said, "Be great in action as you are in thought. Suit the action to the word and the word to the action." In other words, put some work, research, time, and prayer into becoming a good actor.

I have auditioned hundreds of actors and I've seen those who were prepared and those who had only the dream of acting with little preparation. It was obvious they had not taken the time to cultivate, develop, and work at their craft. They relied on their looks or their personality, which can be a plus, but all too quickly becomes not enough when compared to someone with looks, personality, *plus* preparation. Without studying and applying the tools needed to compete in this business there may be moments of success but no longevity.

## Acting Is a Matter of Choices

An acting career is the result of disciplined choices. One of the most important choices you can make is answering the question: what kind of actor can I become? Whether you're just starting out in this business or have been an actor for a while without achieving the success you wanted, ask yourself: Do I have the ...

- **Desire** and **Passion** to act?
- **Energy** and **Stamina** needed by an actor?
- Ability to **Thrive on Uncertainty** required of an actor?
- **Determination** and **Resiliency** necessary to become an actor?

- **Self-Confidence** to be an actor?
- **Spiritual Character** to be faithful to God as an actor?

Author John C. Maxwell states in his book *Talent is Never Enough* a list of what I would call "choices," that I think will be valuable to you if you implement them in your acting career and life.

- Believing lifts you. (Psalms 71:1)
- Passion fuels you. (Isaiah 59:17)
- Focus directs you. (Philippians 3:13)
- Preparation positions you. (Proverbs 16:1-3)
- Practice sharpens you. (Ecclesiastes 10:10)
- Perseverance sustains you. (Romans 5:3-4)
- Courage tests you. (Deuteronomy 31:6)
- Teachability expands you. (Proverbs 14:6, Amp)
- Character protects you. (1 Corinthians 15:33)
- Relationships influence you. (Ephesians 4:14)
- Responsibility strengthens you. (Galatians 6:5)
- Teamwork multiplies you. (1 Corinthians 15:58)

While casting for television and film, I discovered that most *really* good actors make the preceding list of "choices" their lifestyle. I have found these qualities in their acting style and the way they present themselves, not only as actors, but also as people. This list will help you develop your acting career and yourself as a person. It gives you the ability to maximize your talents, gifts, and calling as an actor and child of GOD.

Study the scripture attached to each one of these "choices" to learn beyond any doubt that, "All things work together for good to them that love the LORD and are called according to His purpose" (Romans 8:28). After all, God's Word never returns to Him "void" and He honors His Word above His Name (see Isaiah 55:11, Psalm 138:2).

An incredible amount of effort is required to make acting look effortless! Stay tuned; there's more...

# Your Script for Success

*Whatever you do, wherever you look, your environment must support your goals to help you achieve success as an actor. That includes your relationship with GOD, your networking, your physical environment, your finances, and the way you take care of yourself.*

*Decide that you want it more than you are afraid of it.*

**Bill Cosby ~ Actor**

# DESIRE & PASSION

**L**ike anything worth achieving, embarking on an acting career takes desire and passion. Desire and passion begin with exploration, and you need to begin exploring this industry in many ways. Often, fear can keep us from this process of exploration—stepping into the "unknown." You must learn to defeat fear so that it doesn't rob you of passion and a successful career.

## Passion's Poison — Fear

I've seen many actors with the desire but not the passion it takes to succeed. Sometimes their failure was due to fear. Some of the common fears actors face are:

- Failure
- Fear of auditioning
- Financial hardship
- Rejection
- Stage fright
- Agents and casting directors
- Not being pretty or handsome enough
- Being too young or old

The list could go on and on. No matter what you call it, stage fright or nerves, fear is something that all actors live with but you must be careful that it doesn't become a primary obstacle or an excuse not to pursue your desire and passion. It really does get better; especially the more you audition and the more jobs you book (particularly if the jobs become steady). Fear can be overwhelming and it can create a lack of trust in yourself. For those who have been there, it's a terrible feeling.

## Rechanneling Your Fear

What makes it easier for successful actors—or constantly working actors—is that they have had experience dealing with their nerves before auditions or going on the set; they are used to working under pressure. Dealing with a surge of fear before an audition or performance is about perspective. Successful actors have learned to take that energy and use it as a tool. Fear becomes a motivator for more authentic acting. 2 Timothy 1:7 says, "God has not given you a spirit of fear; but of love, power and of a sound mind." Many Bible versions say a "spirit of timidity" instead of "spirit of fear." Also, other versions may say "self-discipline" in place of "sound mind."

As an actor, if you don't have self-discipline, you will not succeed in this business! The scripture says that GOD

## Desire and Passion

*Desire means "to long for, or to wish for earnestly." Passion means "a strong affection or enthusiasm for an object, concept etc. - such as a passion to act."*

**Passion motivates desire.**

GAVE **YOU** self-discipline—"self-discipline" is your GOD-given gift. There is no excuse, as an actor not to use it! It will drive away many of your fears.

Another thing I found, in my years of casting, is that the actors who combine their desire for acting with a passionate work ethic are the ones who see their desires fulfilled. I believe that you can't separate desire from passion in this business. One can have a desire and do nothing about it, but the person who has the desire and acts on it will see it fulfilled because of their passion. Passion is the motivator of your desires!

## Passion's Partner—Authenticity

Some actors separate their desire from their passion simply because they don't want to work hard enough to have success at their craft. On the other hand, actors who take on the role of storyteller during the audition, who bring truth to imagination, have both desire and passion for this business. Their desire goes deeper than titles, awards, and ego stroking.

The actor with the greatest success in the audition room is the one who has the desire and passion to be a storyteller, not just desperate to be a "Star". All casting directors can sense desperation in an actor during an audition. If your desire and passion to be an actor is motivated merely by money and fame, it will be revealed in your audition and your success rate will probably be low.

If, however, you come to an audition with a clear desire and passion to be a storyteller who brings the character to life, we who watch will be thrilled to see "real acting" and authenticity.

So what will you do today to fulfill and further your desire and passion to be an actor/storyteller? Start by knowing and being your authentic self and receive the gift of self-discipline GOD gave you, and begin counting the cost that will be required.

---

## Your Script for Success

*Never allow fear to get in the way! Instead, let fear become a motivator for more authentic acting.*

*2 Timothy 1:7 says, "God has not given you a spirit of fear or timidity, but of love, power and of self-discipline." (Paraphrased)*

*Any form of art is a form of power; it has impact, it can affect change ... it can not only move us, it makes us move.*

**Ossie Davis ~ Actor**

# ENERGY & STAMINA

There are two words that must become part of every actor's DNA:

*Energy*: a dynamic quality, a positive spiritual flow, a power, force, vigor, liveliness, get-up-and-go, and "oomph."

*Stamina*: staying power, a capacity for continuing without weakening, endurance, resilience, determination, fortitude, and good ol' grit.

As an actor, when you think about the meanings of these words, what do they say to you? Do they give you hope in a business filled with uncertainty, ups and downs, successes and failures? Do the words energy and stamina impart a "never give up" attitude? If not, it should! To be an actor, I believe, these two words must become part of your DNA. In fact, they're required for any aspect of the entertainment business (writer, director, producer, etc.).

When I managed a talent agency years ago, it took a lot of energy and stamina to deal with agents, managers, directors, and producers on television and film sets, plus the efforts involved in auditioning and hiring actors for specific roles. The entertainment industry requires long hours and hard work.

## Love Is the Answer

How do you acquire and maintain the energy and stamina required? The answer is found in a single word — love. You have to fall completely in love with your desire to be an actor. When I fell in love with my wife and began a relationship with her, I wanted to know and experience everything about her and understand what she gave to me and what I could give to her. I wanted to know her personality, her spirit and how she operated. To do that, I spent as much time with her as possible. I never begrudged the effort and stamina required—in fact, I never even considered it work! As an actor, you must begin to see your acting career as a relationship and nurture it as you would any other relationship in your life. Ask yourself, how does my "relationship" with acting make me feel? What work do I need to do to keep this relationship alive, dynamic, growing, and enduring?

## You Don't Need Acting

*The fuller and more complete you are as a person, in mind, body, and spirit, the more attractive you are as an actor. The more interested you become in living your life, the more interesting you become as an actor and as a person. You don't need acting as a means to your identity nor does it make you more lovable, attractive, or interesting. Moreover, you certainly don't need acting to give love to someone or to be loved in return.*

Acting is a creative form but life, and especially life in GOD, is the source of all creativity. Through acting, you can **explore** and **build** your imagination and **develop** the depth of your feelings. However, in life and through your journey with GOD, you **feed** your imagination and

**discover** your depth of feeling. As with any relationship, you still need to have your own identity, your own interests, and a sense of self-worth independent from your partner (acting).

Like a scene you might do in a film or television show, you must focus on your partner in the scene, but you must also know how YOU feel, what YOU think, and what YOU want. If you fail to know who you are, the scene fails. Therefore, to have stamina and energy in this business with all its uncertainties but also its pleasures, you must operate as if you're in a healthy relationship with Acting.

# Your Script for Success

*How do you acquire and maintain the energy and stamina required? The answer is found in a single word —love. You have to fall completely in love with your desire to be an actor; see your acting career as a relationship, and nurture it as you would any other relationship in your life.*

*If we cannot see the possibility of greatness,*
*how can we dream it?*

**Lee Strasberg ~ Acting Coach**

# DETERMINATION & RESILIENCY

I once read, "There is a difference between immediate and ultimate goals. Success with an immediate goal makes it possible to reach the ultimate goal. But failure in the immediate prevents us from reaching our final goal." You must have the determination to never give up on achieving your desire to be the storyteller an actor is supposed to be.

## Determination Requires a Definite Target

There are obstacles an actor must overcome along the way in pursuit of their desire to act in films, television, and on stage. You must make a determination in your heart and mind that you *will* set goals for your career. Goals help you clarify what you want as an actor and goal setting provides you with the steps to get there. Much can be said for actually seeing your goals written down so you can refer to them as often as needed. Creating goals and working toward achieving them will increase your self-confidence and help you be more determined, leading to a satisfying acting career. Having clearly defined goals is actually the quickest way to achieve almost anything in life.

### An Unstoppable Energy Is Activated When You Set a Goal

*A force within you is put in motion when a goal is set and you make a commitment to it. To activate this energy in your career: define your goal~pledge to it~list the steps required~set dates for its completion and write it down.*

The most important thing to understand about goal setting is that goals MUST be written down. Your dream is only a thought and a hope, not a real goal, until you commit it to paper and dedicate yourself to fulfilling it! Many successful people always carry their written goals with them as a reference.

Be proactive: write down your goals and create a plan to work toward them. This strategy is so important to your success that if you find it difficult to do, perhaps you should take advice from a Nike advertising campaign and "Just do it!" Following are tips and warnings for goal setting:

➢ In making your goals, also include family, friends, and physical goals. You need support and stamina to realize your dream!

➢ Make your destiny match your vision by honestly answering these questions:

- Who am I?
- What do I want?
- Where am I going?
- How will I get there?

Don't create goals that are incompatible with one another. Once you create your list of goals, go back through them to make certain they don't contradict each other.

- ➢ Priorities change and so should your goals. What you want this year may not be the same thing you strive for next year. Remember – you have a right to change your mind and edit or completely rewrite your goals!

- ➢ Don't worry yourself over failed goals, such as not getting the number of auditions you want or booking all the jobs you auditioned for. Consider each failure a lesson - a learning experience. Get the positive out of it and appreciate the experience. Use that new information to make certain your goals are sensible and realistic.

- ➢ Above all, pray over your goals and ask the Lord for His input.

Not all actors have the determination and commitment required to set goals for themselves. How much are you willing to commit—enough to set goals? What is your current level of determination? I found that actors who are successful believe they will have success and have the resiliency and determination never to give up on their dream. How far are you willing to go to stand behind your calling to be an actor? Having the determination to fulfill the dream GOD placed in your heart takes a lot of courage and work.

## Resilience Requires Sacrifice

I ask you to consider how much you're willing to commit to becoming a successful actor? The answer is not only how much you're willing to give but also what you are willing to give *up*. There are many sacrifices to be made for those choosing an acting career. Think in advance about what you're willing to give up to have a career. Actors who fail to do this don't prepare themselves for the long-term.

Grasping hold of your determination and remaining resilient, will give you "strength of commitment," a requirement for your acting career. There is always a sacrifice when making a whole-hearted commitment. Consequently, the desired end has to be worth the cost. Resolve, strength of mind, willpower, purpose, fortitude, determination, resilience, and grit—while keeping GOD as your foundation—is the basis for your motivation. It will give you confidence and longevity in your career and cause your acting dreams to develop, thrive, flourish, and come true.

## Dreamers Must Dream

Take time to meditate and daydream about your acting career. This not only brings escape and relaxation, but it provides visions of the future that will inspire and help you to stay focused on your dreams. If you don't naturally believe that *you can* and that *you will* be successful with God's help, I suggest you begin to cultivate a higher belief in yourself and in the power of God in you. Work on it ... dream about it ... believe it every day. Dream while awake! Daydreaming visions of your future will help you find possible solutions to seemingly unsolvable problems, discover inventive ways of developing your career, uncover other creative possibilities, give you time to hear from God, and to review your goals.

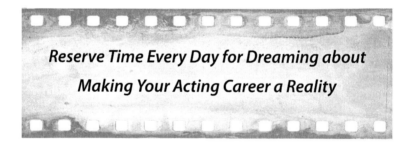

*Reserve Time Every Day for Dreaming about Making Your Acting Career a Reality*

# Your Script for Success

*There is always a sacrifice when making a whole-hearted commitment. Resolve, willpower, purpose, determination, resilience, and grit—while keeping GOD as your foundation—is the basis for your motivation. It will give you confidence and longevity in your career and cause your acting dreams to develop, thrive, flourish, and come true.*

*Getting ahead in a difficult profession requires avid faith in yourself. That is why some people with mediocre talent, but with great inner drive, go so much further than people with vastly superior talent.*

**Sophia Loren ~ Actress**

# SELF-CONFIDENCE

I t may comfort you to know that you're not the only one who needs to find their self-confidence. In fact, some of the most famous and respected actors have had stage fright so badly they threw up before every performance.

What do we know about self-confidence? According to most definitions it's "freedom from doubt; belief in yourself and your abilities to succeed." Self-confidence is usually specific to particular tasks but some people seem to display it in a variety of ways.

Confident actors have a deep faith in their careers. I've observed over years of casting that the best actors know their capabilities. They know they will be able to do what they desire and propose to do (within reason), regardless of obstacles. They even remain confident when they run into "nots" in their career—when some of their goals are not met—like not booking a job, not getting as many auditions as they would like, or not obtaining representation by an agent. Those with self-confidence continue to be positive and believe in themselves. The actors who make the most lasting impression during audition are those who are confident in their ability and are well prepared.

Hebrews 10:35 says, "Therefore do not cast away your confidence, which has great reward …" When you have confidence in your ability as an actor, you know you've prepared yourself fully and you've done your best, how could you NOT believe in yourself? Don't listen to the "voice of doubt" that would tell you, "You're not a good actor" or "You're never going to make it in this business and fulfill the desire GOD has placed in your heart." Choose instead to tune into the voice that says, "If you can see it, you can have it!" "If you can believe you can, … YOU CAN!"

Because self-confidence is a requirement for an acting career, consider this next statement carefully: If you're afraid of rejection and it destroys your self-confidence as an actor, then the entertainment business may not be for you. However, if you are sure this is the direction God is leading you, there are ways to build self-confidence in this business:

1. **IDENTIFY** the things that make you feel unworthy, ashamed, or inferior — identify it, give it a name, and write it down. (Name it and you can defeat it.) A lack of confidence in yourself could be a feeling that you're being judged and can't live up to expectations.

2. **RECOGNIZE** and name your successes. Everyone is good at something, so discover the things at which *you* excel, then focus on your talents. Once you're in this business, give yourself permission to take pride in your auditions and your jobs. Give yourself credit for your successes!

3. **DECREE** and declare that you are "the head and not the tail!" Do not allow yourself to be victimized

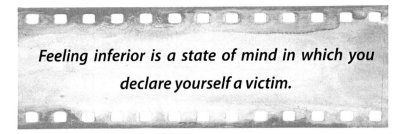

*Feeling inferior is a state of mind in which you declare yourself a victim.*

by stinkin' thinkin'. Find something you enjoy doing and express yourself. Everyone is born with talents and strengths and you can develop and excel in yours. When you're following your passion, it will have a positive effect on you—you'll feel unique and accomplished, which will help build your self-confidence.

4. **BE THANKFUL** for all God has accomplished in you and in your career. Be positive and accept compliments with confidence—simply say, "Thank you."

5. **FAKE IT!** As we say in Hollywood, "Fake it till you make it!" Acting confident can actually make you believe and accept it as true. Pretend that you're a completely self-assured person. Go through the motions and see how you feel! Wow, your first important acting job!

Acting is both an art and a science. The science is obtaining a skill-set by training, studying, and learning the mechanics of acting. The artistic part is taking what you learn, believing in your abilities, and then putting it all together with a part of yourself into a character, using your own interpretation and emotions to form and develop the part.

The famous actor, Johnny Depp, explained it like this, "With any part an actor plays there is a certain amount of themselves in it; there has to be, otherwise it's just not acting, it's lying." The ultimate foundation for self-confidence is knowing that acting is where you are supposed to be "for such a time as this."

*The art form of acting is when an actor brings truth to an imaginary character while backing it up with self-confidence.*

*I have been placed in this job for a purpose, and I am just trying to make great movies and keep my eyes on Him. I don't deserve any praise ... It is definitely all God's hand that I get to do this. And who knows how long this will last? He may choose someone else.*

**Ralph Winter ~ Producer**

# THE SPIRITUAL ASPECT OF ACTING

Jesus taught a fundamental principle of service to others that should be part of our spiritual character. He encouraged us to find God in ourselves and then see Him in everyone else—even our enemies. Once we realize that God wants to use and guide us, we can become integrated into what He has called us to do and see our part in His larger purposes. An acting career encompasses every facet of our life—physical, emotional, mental and, most importantly, spiritual. Each aspect needs to come into alignment with our God-given purpose.

## Try This Exercise

*Sit or stand comfortably, close your eyes and imagine yourself as a single cell in the Body of Christ that is made up of tens of millions of believers. Become centered and focused on the fact that you are one among many who are created for a unique purpose and who have been sent on the quest of fulfillment. Accept the journey before you. Let go of fear, wanting, striving and struggling — become one with that body of believers — merely be who you are, a dearly loved child of your Father God. Remain in that place until you sense the relief and freedom of knowing that you are not in this journey alone. Your brothers and sisters stand alongside you and the Spirit of God and all of Heaven have your back. Listen and hear that whisper in your ear, "I will never leave you or forsake you."*

*You have now created a spiritual place where God is honored. You can return everyday and anytime that you need to become re-centered in who you are and what your life is about!*

## A Spiritual Being on a Human Journey

Stephen Covey, author of many books, gave us an important spiritual perspective on life when he said, "We are not human beings on a spiritual journey, we are spiritual beings on a human journey." Your spiritual journey prepares you; it makes you ready to understand your challenges and begins the adventure of embarking on a career in acting.

Every acting adventure is a quest to discover *something*—the truth about who we are and what we can contribute to our industry. It's easy and comfortable to coast through life but you have received a divine call, uniquely your own. Look back on your call to acting; it may have come through acting in a school play, a dream, a strange encounter, or experience. It could have come from something you read or heard; even the loss of something or someone precious. It may have been something that drastically changed your life or merely through a "knowing" but God placed you in the right place at the right time so that you knew acting was for you!

Perhaps you wanted to refuse the call because it meant facing your greatest fears—I've been there! Years before moving to Los Angeles, a friend asked if I would come to Cincinnati, Ohio, to open a new agency. I had been living in Northern California at the time, working as an agent at a talent agency. Growing up in Ohio, I couldn't recall knowing anyone with a desire to go to Hollywood or a single person with an interest in headshots or auditions! I could only recall cold wintry weather, dreary factories, and bad fashion! For me, going back to Cincinnati was a journey into a great fear, my fear of the unknown. Now that I no longer live there, I can tell you that it was a wonderful learning experience and the "spirit of Hollywood" lives strongly even in Cincinnati. Saying yes and going back to Ohio prepared me for what I would face years later as a casting director in Hollywood.

An actor creates their character for a role the same way that you create your spiritual character—from the inside. Finding your spiritual character's journey is the pathway to discovering your life and your spirit. It's the doorway to knowing the heart of God for you. Your spiritual journey is not about *having,* it's simply about *being* and life is certainly not going to be boring.

Some individuals may see Hollywood as a way out of their struggles but if that's what you see, it's not what you'll get! It's important to stop and consider the cost of your *spiritual* journey and your *spiritual* character as you contemplate pursuing an acting career. For some actors, these costs will total far more than any dollar amount spent pursuing the industry. There can be costs in your relationships, to your physical and mental health, and to your spirit. Yet despite the cost, most actors would never choose any other way of life. However, without the strong foundation of your spiritual walk with GOD, which must always come first, being an actor can be quite empty. Don't get me wrong, you can have great, rewarding and exciting times as an actor—the audition process, booking the job, going to the premiere of your film, walking the Red Carpet, and getting applause for a job well done—however, those things are never enough those things are never enough in and of themselves. The most successful actors have a strong spiritual character and a good sense of who they are.

Taking all of this into account, spend some time reflecting on the following: *Is your spiritual character strong enough to maintain what it takes to survive in this business?*

## Hollywood's Spiritual Battles

An actor will face a host of spiritual battles. Some are within yourself and others from people in the industry. Ephesians 6:12 explains spiritual battles by saying:

> For we do not wrestle against flesh and blood, but against principalities, against powers, against the rulers of the darkness of this age, against spiritual host of wickedness in the heavenly places.

Everything in the visible or physical realm is caused, provoked, or at least influenced by something in the invisible or spiritual realm.

I could have written chapters for this book on how to audition, the kinds of training needed to be an actor, how to get an agent, or how to survive as an actor in Hollywood, and other practical tips. You will find that information in the manual I co-authored, *XP Acting 101- Practical Training for Actors*; but that is not the focus of *this* book. If you're not well grounded in your walk with GOD and aware of the subtle tactics of your enemy to kill, steal, and destroy you—spiritually, mentally, and physically— no tips will help you. Some of the strongest spirits I encountered during my years in Hollywood were narcissism, intimidation, mammon, fear, insecurity, loneliness, doubt, and immorality.

## Spirit of Narcissism

Narcissism is a huge spirit in the entertainment industry. It is "all about me" and what you think about me. Actors beware! Some actors are so full of themselves and so self-absorbed that you can barely hold a conversation with them. I've tried many times to have conversations with actors who can only speak their "verbal acting resume." What is a verbal acting resume? It's a detailed recitation of *their* work, who *they* are currently training with, what project *they* are currently shooting, or complaints about *their* agent, or *their* lack of acting jobs.

At times, I have wished an actor could talk "off camera" about other aspects of their life and could say something other than, "Can I audition for you sometime" or "Can you look at my headshot?" This form of self-idolatry sucks the life out of the person listening. Don't get me wrong, an actor should be self-promoting on some level, for instance during an interview with a casting director, director or producer.

Narcissism is destructive to a career because it makes you unappealing to the very people with whom you would like to work. One of the best little books on this subject, which I recommend to all present and future actors and for that matter to everyone else, is titled *Overcoming the Spirit of Narcissism* by Patricia King.

Ultimately, the narcissism in Hollywood separates people from one another, creating a sense of isolation and feeling of loneliness. Although narcissism is found in any career, the Hollywood narcissist can be easily spotted. The spirit of narcissism includes egotism, vanity, conceitedness, indulgence in self-love, illusions of grandiosity, or simple selfishness. When applied to a social group such as actors and others associated with the business, it leads to elitism and an indifference to the plight of others.

How do Christians overcome narcissism? A friend of mine, Melanie Wistar, who has been in "the business" for over 14 years as a writer for television and film, teaches a screenwriting workshop that I recently attended. Melanie made a statement that created an "aha" moment in my life. Okay, get ready—it can change your thinking about Kingdom work and defeating narcissism. I quote, "We are all in this together ... there is PLENTY to go around in God's kingdom ... we're ALL called by Him." Proverbs 22:2 says it like this, "Rich and poor have this in common: the LORD is the maker of them all."

## The Spirits of Loneliness, Doubt, & Discouragement

Loneliness can easily sneak into an actor's life. Most actors I know, both the very successful and those on their way, all go through devastating times of loneliness. Actors have left their hometowns, family, friends, and perhaps local success as an actor to pursue a dream.

Commonly upon arriving in Hollywood, your studio apartment is adorned with photos of friends and family that you received at a going away party; a few posters of your favorite movies; and a cupboard full of Ramen Noodles. Coming home from a long day at a job that has nothing to do with acting but is flexible enough to allow you to go on auditions, or even coming home from an audition, you open the door wishing that someone was waiting with a comforting hug.

During these times of frustration and loneliness, it's very important to create a *spiritual sanctuary* where you can reside; a place for your quiet time with GOD, praise & worship, or uplifting music ready at the push of a button. This is also the time to review your goals and remember that you're not in this alone. Perhaps it is time to return to the spiritual sanctuary you built in the earlier exercise.

Some days you may feel like Dorothy in the Wizard of Oz, as she was caught up in that great Kansas tornado—the noise … the whirlwind … the grasping for something to hold on to … your cry for help and then finding yourself in Oz, or Hollywood. The strange land that is the entertainment capital of the world, crowded with masses of people, confusing freeways, bright lights, cameras, award ceremonies, the Red Carpet, paparazzi, and interviews—you get the picture? If you ever get to experience this in your acting career, there can and will be times when you wake up the next morning after all the excitement to feel troubled, bitter, agitated, angry, and impatient. These feelings may come from a variety of reasons, such as: no auditions, your agent has not booked you any jobs lately, your finances are low, and there is no one with whom to share your feelings and frustrations about what you're going through. At those times, you see your problems as greater than God's ability (or willingness) to bring the solutions. Lacking faith in His goodness, you can't trust that God is the source for all your needs!

Loneliness, without faith and hope in your relationship with GOD, can become paralyzing and lead to deeper attacks such as depression and anxiety. It can creep in unaware and, if not dealt with, it can ultimately stop your acting career.

Ben Stein, an American writer, actor, lawyer, and commentator on political and economic issues said, "It is inevitable that some defeat will enter even the most victorious life. The human spirit is never finished when it is defeated; it is finished when it surrenders."

Jesus encourages us with a no-nonsense assessment of what we can expect in life in John 16:33:

> I have told you these things so that in me you may
> have peace. In this world you will have trouble.
> But take heart! I have overcome the world.

Actors often doubt themselves; however, most of us entertain uncertainty when we try something new. In fact, almost everyone is in some way plagued with doubts of some kind. Doubts can be beneficial at times. You can doubt your approach to your goals and seek to improve them but you can't let your doubts keep you from your ultimate goal of having a successful acting career. Many people find taking risks difficult and scary. It is better to take a risk than to let your doubts prevent you from trying at all. Don't let doubt stop you from taking risks in your career.

## Overpowering Your Spiritual Enemies

Belief is the enemy of doubt, so learning to think positively and believing in your ability to be successful is a vital first step. Remember, you will succeed if you think you will or fail if that's what you believe. Your thoughts are self-fulfilling prophecies so you must control your thought life and put a stop to negative thinking.

Likewise, never pay heed to people who would discourage you about your career, whose words plant doubts in you. They can be wolves in sheep's clothing (which sadly may include both family and friends). Keep yourself in the company of people whose thoughts and attitudes toward life in general and acting in particular are positive.

Proverbs 27:19 says, "As a face is reflected in water, so the heart reflects the person." To me this means that what you put into your heart and mind defines your character and influences the person you are. Keep in mind that you *will* experience doubt in yourself as an actor, everyone does, it's part of the acting life. There will be times when failure fills your mind with doubt and it's hard to muster confidence; yet, you cannot let go of your commitment, no matter how shaken you are by doubt. In fact, any setback should only prompt you to double your resolve to make another attempt to reach your goal.

Train your mind to build your self-control and self-confidence—every step towards self-confidence helps you to rid your mind of doubt. Healthy doubt can be helpful in gaining wisdom and improving your approach to achieving advancement in life and in acting. However, when doubt causes depression and inactivity, or stands like a mountain blocking your way to your destination, it's time to go back to your reasons for acting. You can draw strength from the fact that GOD placed it in your heart to act and He will make a way. You must strengthen your will to succeed at all costs and weaken doubt by all possible means to lead a life of fulfillment.

Know that you're right where you're supposed to be. Doubt can also serve to remind us that we must grow more in our faith.

## Your Script for Success

*Become well grounded in your walk with GOD and aware of the subtle tactics of your enemy to kill, steal, and destroy you—spiritually, mentally, and physically. Draw strength from the fact that GOD placed it in your heart to act and He will make a way.*

*I meditate and pray all the time. The faith and respect that I have in the power of God in my life is what I've used to keep myself grounded, and it has allowed me to move away from the storms that were in my life. I'm still a work in progress, but I know that as long as I stay close to God I'll be all right.*

**Halle Berry ~ Actress**

# DECREES FOR THE ACTOR

O ne of the most important things you can do is make place in your life for a regular "quiet time" with GOD. It should be a time when you not only communicate with Him but also articulate the declarations and affirmations God is speaking over you.

Many actors recite positive affirmations to help build their confidence before auditions and performances, or just to keep their faith strong for their acting career. I have created decrees for Kingdom-minded actors who desire to strengthen their faith. I believe that if you will confess everyday who you are in GOD, using His Word as your source, you will have great success. Christians who live defeated lives are overcome because they believe and confess wrong things. In Proverbs, it states that, "life and death are in the power of the tongue." Confessions have power in both the physical and spiritual universe.

## What You Say Is What You Empower

Declarations are so powerful that GOD never does anything without saying it first—He spoke the world into existence. He spoke and told you to fulfill your dream to become an actor and He encourages you to risk failure by promising, "I will never leave you nor forsake you" (Hebrews 13:5).

The principles of faith are based on spiritual laws that work for anyone who applies them and we put them into action with our words. If Jesus came to you and said, "Starting today, everything you say about your acting career and about yourself as an actor will come to pass," would that change what you say about yourself and your career?

Although He may never tell you that personally, He said in Job 22:28:

> You will also declare a thing, and it will be established for you; So light will shine on your ways (NKJV).

In addition to their spiritual impact, the words you speak program your spirit and mind for either success or failure.

Faith comes much more quickly when you quote, hear, and speak decrees from God's Word. There is creative power in confessing and decreeing Scripture over yourself. As you begin to believe the things God's Word says about you and for you, a new level of faith will arise. Your decrees and confession can set in motion the plans God has for you and the provision you need to become the actor He called you to be.

The following decrees from the Word of God can change how you live your acting life. My prayer is that as an actor you will live out your life with authenticity and faithfulness to your God-given calling.

Jesus lived His life with the awareness that God was up to something important on the earth and that anyone could be a part of it. He inspired, challenged, comforted, and invited people to be open to what God was doing in that day and the same thing is happening in our day.

Always remain open to God's leading in the process of your career. God is always drawing and inviting us to open our eyes to understand more fully and join Him in what He is doing. Be blessed and be a blessing!

The well-known teacher and minister, Dr. Robert Schuller, always spoke the following blessing over his congregation, and I want to pronounce the same blessing upon you:

> "And now may the Lord bless you and keep you. May the Lord make His face to shine upon you and be gracious unto you. And may God give you His peace in your going out and in your coming in, in your lying down and in your rising up, in your labor and in your leisure, in your laughter and in your tears ... Until you come to stand before Jesus in that day in which there is no sunset and no dawning. Amen."

# DECREES FOR THE ACTOR

*Read aloud the following scriptures that have been*
*personalized especially for you.*

For God has not given me a spirit of fear and timidity, but of power, love, and self-discipline (2 Timothy 1:7).

God has great plans for me: plans for good and not for disaster, they give me a future and a hope (Jeremiah 29:11).

The Lord will perfect that which concerns me (Psalm138:8).

I commit my actions to the Lord, and my plans will succeed (Proverbs 16:3).

I can and I will do all things through Christ who gives me strength (Philippians. 4:13).

I trust in the Lord with all my heart and do not depend on my own understanding. In all my ways, I acknowledge Him and He directs my path (Proverbs 3:5).

When I am afraid, I put my trust in God (Psalm 56:3).

In YOU, O Lord, do I put my trust and confidently take
 refuge; let me never be put to shame or confusion
(Psalm 71:1 Amp).

I will never be disgraced because I trust in God. Disgrace
comes to those who try to deceive others (Psalm 25:3).

For God is working in me, giving me the desire and the
power to do what pleases Him (Philippians 2:13).

I am filled with the knowledge of the Lord's will in all
wisdom and spiritual understanding (Colossians 1:9).

I praise God for what He has promised. I trust in God, so
why should I be afraid? What can mere mortals do to me
(Psalm 56:4)?

I am of God and will overcome. For greater is He that is
in me, than he that is in the world (1 John 4:40).

I am far from oppression and fear does not come near me
(Isaiah. 54:14).

I am a doer of the Word of God and I am blessed in my deeds. I am happy in those things which I do because I am a doer of the Word of God (James 1:22).

I delight myself in the Lord and He gives me the desires of my heart (Psalms. 119:25).

There is no lack, for my God supplies all my needs according to His riches in glory by Christ Jesus (Philippians 4:19).

God is on my side. He is in me now; who can be against me? He has given to me all things that pertain to life and godliness. Therefore, I am a partaker of His divine nature (2 Corinthians 6:16; John 10:10; 2 Peter 1:3-4; Romans 8:31).

I will decree a thing, and it shall be established to me; and the light shall shine upon my ways (Job. 22:28).

The LORD will keep watch over me as I come and as I go, both now and forever (Psalm 121:8).

# SCOTT LAIRSON

## *Casting Director*

Scott is a graduate of Oral Roberts University with a Bachelor's Degree in Telecommunications. His experience in dealing with talent began with his role as a Road Manager and Booking Agent for Carman Ministries Music Corporation when he was one of the top Christian solo artists in the country.

Since 1993 Scott Lairson has worked as a casting director in Hollywood. He worked on the Emmy Award winning NYPD Blue seven seasons. He assisted in casting various Steven Bochco Productions such as "Brooklyn South", "City of Angels", "NYPD 2069," "Marriage," "Philly" and "Blind Justice." He also worked on "Star Trek Voyager", "Deep Space 9", "Desperate Housewives", and many television pilots and feature films.

Scott has cast the independent features "A Wonderous Fate," "Tattered Angel," featuring Linda Carter, and short features, "Innocent," "God's Helper," and "Meant To Be."

Scott was also an agent in San Francisco, acting as a liaison to clients such as Proctor & Gamble, Wendy's, and The Limited.

Originally from Cincinnati, Ohio, Scott currently lives in the Phoenix area with his wife, Pat and is an acting instructor for XPMEDIA in Maricopa, Arizona.

His passion is to see the television and film industry filled with the life and light of the Kingdom of God.

**Scott can be contacted at scott@xpacting.com**

Available at the "Store" at **XPmedia.com.**

# Break this Destructive Pattern!

Author Patricia King delves into the psychological and spiritual roots of narcissism. You will learn what narcissism is and how it manifests, how it takes root in an individual, the truth about narcissism in the church today, how to live with someone who is under of influence of a spirit of narcissism, and more!

### Stop the Bully!

Patricia King and Family Counselor Pat Lairson expose the bully. Bullies can strike in seconds at school or work, in cyberspace, or even at home. But that negative experience can be turned into its opposite, a life changing positive. In this book, you will find all the answers you need to understand and overcome bullying, to protect yourself and your loved ones.

### Decrees Inspired by the Psalms

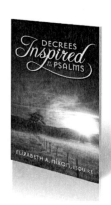

As a practicing lawyer, Elizabeth A. Nixon is familiar with the legal authority behind decrees and she skillfully unpacks biblical and practical insights regarding their importance. 43 decrees are offered, including Decrees for the Seven Mountains or spheres of influence, inspired by Psalm 24.

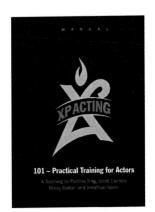

Additional copies of this book
and other book titles from
XP media  and XP Publishing
are available at **XPmedia.com**

## BULK ORDERS:

We have bulk/wholesale prices for stores and ministries. Please contact: usaresource@xpmedia.com and the resource manager will help you.

For Canadian bulk orders please contact:
resource@xpmedia.com

**www.XPpublishing.com**

**A Ministry of Patricia King and
Christian Services Association**